Arnold Schwarzenegger

Julia Holt

JAMESTOWN PUBLISHERS
a division of NTC/Contemporary Publishing Group
Lincolnwood, Illinois USA

Acknowledgments
Cover photo:
© Harry Langdon

Photos:
Page iv, 4, & 7 © Michael Montfort/Shooting Star Int'l
Page 10 © Tri–Star/Shooting Star Int'l
Page 12 © Universal/Shooting Star
Page 14 © Ron Davis/Shooting Star Int'l
Page 18 © Laura D. Luongo/Shooting Star

First published in United Kingdom by Hodder & Stoughton
Educational in Association with the Basic Skills Agency.

ISBN: 0-89061-422-9

Published by Jamestown Publishers,
a division of NTC/Contemporary Publishing Group, Inc.
4255 West Touhy Avenue,
Lincolnwood (Chicago), Illinois 60646–1975 U.S.A.

Manufactured in the United States of America.

8 9 0 VP 0 9 8 7 6 5 4 3 2 1

REAL LIVES

Arnold Schwarzenegger

Contents

	Page
Beginning	1
First Career	3
Second Career	6
Women	15
Third Career	17
Fourth Career?	19

Beginning

Arnold Schwarzenegger
has come a long way
from his beginnings.

He is a household name,
a famous film star,
and one of the best paid actors
in the world.

He has had three successful careers—
not bad for a poor boy
from a small Austrian village.

Arnold Schwarzenegger
had a difficult childhood.

He was born in July 1947
in a village near Graz in Austria.

The family was poor.
His mother had to bring water
from a fountain outside.
They could only afford meat
once a week.

His father was the police chief
and was very strict
with Arnold and his elder brother.

His elder brother was the favorite.

First Career

Arnold wanted to find a way
to be as strong as his father.

He had big dreams.
He knew he would be a success.

At 15 he started training
to be a body builder.
He became dedicated
to this art form.

He built his body
to look like the superheroes
in comic books.

In 1965
he had one year in the army.
He was a tank driver.

The army fed him meat every day,
and so he grew even more.

At eighteen
he was Junior Mr. Universe.

Two years later
he became Mr. Universe.

He had 22-inch arms,
and a 57-inch chest.

Arnold went on
to win this competition
another four times.

He also won
the Mr. Olympia competition
seven times.

But he knew that body building
was not a job for life,
and so he had to find
his next career.

Second Career

In 1968 Arnold was in America.
He was training for a competition
when he was given a part
in a film about body building.

The film was *Pumping Iron.*

He went on to star
in some of the most successful films
ever made.

Conan the Barbarian in 1982
was his next big hit.

It was a fantasy film
full of sword fights
and Arnold's muscles.

Two years later he made a follow-up,
called *Conan the Destroyer.*

Both films made over $100 million.

Arnold was now
a household name.

He became rich,
but he looked after his money.
He had not forgotten
the days when he had none.

Two years later
came an even bigger hit,
The Terminator.

He played a robot killer
sent from the future
to kill the female star of the film.

All Schwarzenegger's fantasy films
are about good versus evil.

The famous line "I'll be back"
came from *The Terminator.*

Later Arnold made *Terminator 2.*
This time the robot was on the side of good.

Arnold has not won any awards
for his acting,
but he has made a lot of money
from his films.

His pay for *Terminator 2*
was a $9 million jet plane.

His other big action films are:

Commando, 1985
The Predator, 1987
The Running Man, 1987
Total Recall, 1990
Last Action Hero, 1993
True Lies, 1995
The Eraser, 1996

In 1996 Arnold made another Terminator film.
This one is very special
because it is in 3D.

You can only watch this film
with special glasses,
and you can only see it
at Universal Studios in America.

Arnold has also made comedy films.

In these films
his size is used as a joke.

In *Kindergarten Cop*
he acts with small children.
In *Twins* he plays the twin of Danny DeVito.

His films are more popular
than Clint Eastwood's
or Sylvester Stallone's.

In 1994 he grew even bigger
when he played a pregnant man.

The film was called *Junior,*
and Danny DeVito was the midwife.

Arnold said he learned so much
from watching his wife
when she was pregnant.

Women

Arnold Schwarzenegger
has had plenty of girlfriends,
but only three serious ones.

He met Maria Shriver in 1977,
when he was living with another woman.

He married Maria nine years later.

Maria was a newscaster
and is part of the Kennedy family.

She is a very rich woman
from money left to her
by her family.

Maria, Arnold, and their two girls
lived in Hollywood
in a house with seven bedrooms.

But in 1993, when their son was born,
Arnold also bought the house next door
for three million dollars.

He put in a new basketball court
for his baby son.

Then he bought the house next door to that.
So now they have
fifteen bedrooms!

Third Career

Schwarzenegger is not all muscle.
He has a head for business.

His last films
have not been big money makers.
So now he fights more
in the business world
than he does in films.

His third career is being a business man.

He owns many buildings
including a chain of cafés
(they are called Planet Hollywood,
and Arnold owns them with Sylvester Stallone).
He also owns a chain of gyms
and many shops and houses.

He is still making lots of money.
His third career is going very well.

Fourth Career?

Arnold became
an American citizen in 1983.

Some people say
he wants to be in politics.

He says,
"I set out to be the best,
and I am."

Will his fourth career be in politics?
Will he be a politician in Washington one day?

No matter what Arnold Schwarzenegger does,
he won't stay out of the spotlight for long.

He'll be back.